C++ PROGRAMMING FOR BEGINNERS

A Simple Start To C++ Programming Written By A Software Engineer

SCOTT SANDERSON

Contents

1

C++ Basics

C++ is an object-oriented language, which derives most of its features and base constructs from C. This is perhaps the reason why C++ is known as a 'superset' of C. Any program written in the C programming language is legally and syntactically an ANSI C++ program. However, the reverse of this statement is not true. Without dwelling into a lot of theory, let us directly move on to programming, which is certainly the best way to learn any programming language.

A Basic C++ Program

The simplest program to start with is one that prints 'Hello World' on the screen. The code for this program is given below:

Code:

```
//Simple C++ Program
#include <iostream>
using namespace std;
int main ()
{
cout << "Hello World!";
```

```
return 0;
}
```

Output:

Hello World!

Before moving any further, let us analyze this program line-by-line. The first line is the comments line. This line is not included in the actual code, which is run by the machine. It is only for developers to reference at a later time and make understanding of the code easier. There are two ways of writing comments in C++. One of these methods uses '//' before the text and the other one uses '/*' before the text and '*/' at the terminating end.

The second line uses a #include and includes iostream library to the code. This library facilitates input-output operations and allows the user to use console for giving input and getting output. The third statement specifies that the code is using the namespace std. The std namespace contains all the inbuilt libraries of the C++ package. Therefore, if you are hoping to use any these libraries, then it is essential for you to include this statement.

The program for printing 'Hello World!' begins with the fourth statement. The function, main(), is the function from where execution begins in C++ programming language. It is mandatory for the main() to return an integer value. The scope of the function is described using curly braces, '{' and '}'.

The body of the function contains two statements. The first statement uses a standard I/O operation cout, which is used for printing the specified output on the screen. A similar function, cin, is used for taking input from the console. While, the operation, cout, uses '<<' operator, cin operation uses '>>' operator. The next statement returns an integer value, as previously mentioned.

Both the statements are terminated with a semicolon

(;), which is a C++ standard. However, this rule does not apply to directives like *include*. It is important to note here that C++ is not format specific. Therefore, you can write all the statements one-after-another, separated by semicolons, in the same line. Giving a proper structure to the program makes it more readable and easy to understand.

Please note that the instructions for writing, editing, compiling and running a program are compiler-dependent. You may use Dev-C++ or Turbo C if you are using Windows and any GCC compiler for Unix/Linux or Mac.

2

Data Types, Variables and Constants

While the program illustrated in the previous chapter is rather simple and with questionable usefulness, it should have laid the required foundation to get started with C++ programming. Quite obviously, programming is not just limited printing texts on the console. In fact, it is much more complicated than that. As we dwell into the complexities of this programming language, the first thing to look at is variables.

As a kid, when you learned addition and subtraction, your teacher or parents must have asked you to keep one number in your memory, and then memorize the second number. Once you have the two numbers, you must add them and memorize the result. When we mention the operation 'memorize', we are actually referring to a variable in the context of the computer.

Therefore, a variable can simply be described as a memory cell that saves a defined value. For example, if you go back to the example of addition, then you can assume two cells, '*a*' and '*b*', which contain the values to be added.

A result called '*result*' shall contain the added value. Therefore, a, b and result are variables.

Identifiers

It is difficult to memorize memory cell addresses and refer to them every time you wish to perform an operation on the same. In order to solve this issue, the concept of identifiers was introduced. An identifier is a name given to the memory cell with the defined value, while it is declared. Any changes, made to the value of this memory cell, are performed using the associated identifier. In the previous example, the names, 'a', 'b' and 'result' are identifiers.

The identifiers used as names for variables should also be valid. There are several guidelines that determine if an identifier is valid or not, which are as follows:

1. Should be a sequence of letter, numbers and underscores (_).
2. Should not contain spaces, symbols or punctuation marks.
3. Should begin with an underscore or letter.
4. Should not start with a number.
5. Should not be a reserved keyword. A list of reserved keywords is provided at the end of the chapter in Appendix I.

Please note that some compilers may not support keywords starting with underscore. They are reserved for usage by the compiler itself. Also, C++ is case-sensitive. Therefore, x and X are two different variables. So, be careful!

Fundamental Data Types

Gong back to the example of addition, you inherently know that you are memorizing two integers. This is not the case with the computer as you need to explicitly declare everything before any processing can take place. Therefore, you need to tell the computer which type of data you are going to store in the variable concerned. It is only after this declaration that the computer assigns memory to the variable.

The table given below shows the fundamental data types, their memory requirements and a brief description of what they entail. However, please note that the memory size is machine and system dependent. The values given in the table are true for a standard 32-bit machine.

Data Type

Memory Required

Descriptions

char

1 byte

Any character

short int

or

short

2 bytes

Short Integer

int

4 bytes

Standard integer

long int

or

long

4 bytes

Long integer

float

4 bytes

Floating point number

double

8 bytes

Double precision floating point number
long double
8 bytes
Long double precision floating point number
bool
1 byte
Boolean
wchar_t
2 bytes/4 bytes
Wide character

Declaration of Variables

A variable can be declared using the following statement:

<data type> <identifier>

Example:

int a;

This statement declares that the variable a will contain integer values. There can be several variations of this statement. You can define the variable in the following manner using the same statement.

int a = 0;

This declaration assigns the value 0 to the variable a.

In addition, you can also declare several variables using the same statement. An example is given below:

int a, b, c;

In this case, all the variables, a, b and c, are declared to be integers.

Integers (int, short and long) can be declared as signed or unsigned. You need to use the keywords *signed* and *unsigned* in the statement in the following manner:

signed int a;

or

unsigned int a;

In the absence of the keyword, the system assumed

that the variable is signed in nature. You can also use the keywords *signed* and *unsigned* with char. If you use *unsigned char,* then you can only store characters in the variable. However, if you use signed char, you can store integers, one byte long, in the variable.

Scope of Variables

As a rule, you can use a variable only after you have declared it. In addition to this, there exists a concept of 'scope'. Scope is of two types: global and local. A variable is said to have global scope if the variable is declared outside the body of the code. As a result, this variable is available to all the functions of the program.

Any variable declared inside the body of the code is inevitably local in nature and has local scope. The scope limitation of the variable is the block in which the variable is present, which is defined by enclosed braces, '{' and '}'.

Initialization of Variables

When you declare a variable, it contains garbage value. In other words, the value of the variable cannot be predicted. In order to make the variable usable and useful, you need to define it by assigning a value to the same. Initialization of a variable can be done via two methods.

According to the first method, the variable must be defined at the time of its declaration.

Standard format:

<type identifier> <variable> = <value>

Sample implementation:

int a = 0;

The other type of initialization makes use of the constructor method.

Standard format:

<type identifier> <variable>(value)

Sample implementation:

int a(0);

Strings

Strings are a data type, which is used to store non-numerical values. The length and number of values is equal to or greater than 1. The C++ standard library supports '*Strings*' data type. However, in order to use the functionality included in the library, you must include the header file, string, in the following manner.

#include<string>

Strings can be declared and defined in the following manner:

string name = "John";

An alternate method for accomplishing the same task is:

string name;

name = "John"

Constants

Expressions that contain a fixed value are called constants.

Literals

Literals are used to denote concrete values inside the source code. For instance, the integers assigned to variables like 0, in the previous example, is a literal. There are several types of literal constants, which are described in the section to follow.

Integer Numerals

They are numerical constants that distinguish between the decimal qualities of a number. Recognize that, in order to express a numerical constant, we don't need to use any exceptional character or quotes. Whenever, we write 1871 in a system, we will be alluding to the worth 1871.

Notwithstanding decimal numbers (those that every one of us have utilized consistently), C++ permits the utilization as strict constants of octal numbers (base 8) and hexadecimal numbers (base 16). On the off chance that we need to express an octal number, we need to place a 0 (zero character) before it. Besides this, with a specific end goal to express a hexadecimal number, we need to place the characters 0x (zero, x) before the number.

Literal constants, in the same way as variables, are considered to have a particular type. Of course, number literals are of sort int. In any case, we can drive them to either unsigned form by attaching the u character to it, or long form by annexing l. In both cases, the postfix could be determined utilizing either upper or lowercase letters.

Floating Point Literals

These literals express numbers in the form of exponents and numbers. They can incorporate a decimal point, an e character (symbolic of exponent), where a number occurs after the e character. Moreover, a number may have both a decimal point and an e character.

Examples:

3.14159 / 3.14159

6.02e23 / 6.02 x 10^23

1.6e-19 / 1.6 x 10^-19

In the preceding examples, it can be seen how floating-point numbers are written. The first illustration uses decimal point whereas the last two numbers use e character to indicate a 10^x, where x is the degree of exponentiation. 'Double' is the default type, used for floating point representation.

Character and String Literals

Non-numerical constants also exist in C++. While a character is a single char, a string represents a string of characters. Recognize that to speak of a solitary character, we wall it in the middle of single quotes ('). On the other hand, to express a string (which for the most part comprises of more than one character), we wall it in the middle of double quotes (").

Boolean Literals

There are just two legitimate Boolean literals: false and true. These could be communicated in C++ as estimations of type bool by utilizing the Boolean literals false and true.

Defined Constants (#define)

You can characterize your names for constants that you utilize all the time without needing to depend on memory-expending variables, just by utilizing the #define preprocessor order.

The syntax for the same is as follows:

#define <identifier> <value>

Example:

#define EXP 10

The #define mandate is not a C++ explanation. However, it is an order for the preprocessor. In this manner, it accepts the whole line as the order and does not oblige a semicolon (;) at its end. In the event that you add a semicolon character (;) at the end, it will likewise be added in all events inside the group of the program that the preprocessor substitutes.

Declared Constants (const)

You can pronounce constants with a particular sort in the same route, as you would do with a variable, using the const keyword. Here, tabulator and pathwidth are two written constants. They are dealt with much the same as standard variables aside from the fact that their qualities can't be altered after their definition.

3

Operators

When we know of the presence of variables and constants, we can start to work with them. In order to facilitate processing on these variables and constants, operators are provided by the C++ programming language. Not at all like different programming languages in which operators are basically essential words, administrators in C++ are for the most part made of signs that are not included in the letter set yet are accessible in all consoles. This makes C++ code shorter and more global, since it depends less on English words, yet obliges a tad bit of learning exertion initially.

Assignment (=)

This operator assigns a value to a variable.

Syntax:

<variable identifier> = <value>

Example:

x = 0;

This announcement relegates the number value 5 to the variable a. The part at the left of the operator (=) is known as the rvalue (right value) and the right one as the lvalue (left value). The lvalue must be a variable though the rvalue might be either a constant, a variable or any mixture of these. The most vital tenet when allocating is the right-to-left operation is that the operation dependably happens from right to left, and never the other way.

Syntax:

<lvalue> = <rvalue>;

Example:

x = y;

This announcement doles out to variable x (lvalue) the value contained in variable y (rvalue). A property that C++ has over other programming languages is that the task operation could be utilized as the rvalue (or part of a rvalue) for an alternate task operation.

Example:

x = 7 + (y = 0);

In this example statement, 0 is allocated to variable y and then add 7 to this value. The result is assigned to x.

The accompanying statement is additionally legitimate in C++:

x = y = z = 0;

It relegates 0 to the all the three variables: x, y and z.

The five arithmetical operations upheld by the C++ dialect are: add (+), subtract (-), multiply (*), division (/) and modulo (%). The stand out that you may not be so used to see is modulo. This operator gives remainder of division as the result. For example, if you perform the following operation:

a = 21 % 4;

The remainder of the division of 21 with 4 is 1. This is the output of this operation.

Compound Assignment

Compound operators include subtraction (-=), addition (+=), division (/=), multiplication (*=), >>=, <<= and modulo (%=). In addition to bitwise logical operators can also be used. When we need to adjust the estimation of a variable by performing an operation on its present, compound assignments can be used.

Syntax:

<variable identifier><operator> = <value>

Example:

x+ = 1

In the example shown above, the value of x is incremented by 1.

Increase and Decrease (++, --)

In an attempt to reduce the number of statements used, operations increase and decrease are provided. These statements are equivalent to +=1 and to -=1, respectively.

In the early C compilers, the three past articulations presumably delivered distinctive executable code relying upon which one was utilized. These days, this sort of code streamlining, is done by the compiler, accordingly the three interpretations ought to deliver precisely the same executable code.

A normal for this operation is that it might be utilized both as a prefix and as a postfix. That implies that it could be composed either before the variable identifier (++a) or after it (a++). Albeit in basic statements like a++ or ++a, both have precisely the same importance. However, in different declarations in which the consequence of the build or abatement operation is assessed as a worth in an external interpretation, they may have a vital distinction in their significance.

In the case that the increment operation is utilized as a prefix (++a) the value is incremented before the consequence of the statement is assessed and subsequently the expanded worth is considered in the external outflow. On the off chance that that it is utilized as a postfix (a++), the value is expanded in the wake of being assessed and accordingly the value put away before the build operation is assessed in the external representation.

Relational and Equality Operators

These operators include not equal to (!=), equality (==), lesser than (<),lesser than and equal to (<=), greater than (>) and greater than or equal to (>=).

To assess an examination between two interpretations we can utilize the relational and correspondence operations. The consequence of a relational operation is a Boolean value. This result can have one of the two values: false or true.

We may need to look at two interpretations, for instance, to know whether they are equivalent or if one is more noteworthy than the other is. Here is a rundown of the operators that could be utilized within C++:

Example:

(7 == 3) //This expression evaluates to false
(6 > 5) //This expression evaluates to true
(3 != 4) //This expression evaluates to true
(6 >= 6) //This expression evaluates to true
(5 < 5) //This expression evaluates to false

Logical Operators

C++ programming language supports three logical operations namely, not (!), and (&&) and or (| |).

The Operator not (!) is the C++ administrator to perform the Boolean operation NOT. It has one and only operand, and the main thing that it does is to converse the value of it. If the value of the operand is true, then it is converted to false. On the other hand, if the value is false, the same is converted to true. Essentially, it furnishes a proportional payback Boolean benefit of assessing its operand.

The other two operations, && and | |, make use of two

variables. The operation and (&&) relates with Boolean sensible operation AND. This operation results in true if and only if both the operands are true. On the other hand, the operation || compares with Boolean operation OR and results in a true value if at least one of the two operands is true.

Conditional Operator (?)

This operator assesses a declaration giving back a value if that outflow is true and an alternate one if the statement is assessed as false.

Syntax:

conditionForTesting ? resultIfTrue : resultIfFalse

If conditionForTesting is true, the statement will return resultIfTrue. However, if the conditionForTesting is false, then it will return resultIfFalse.

Comma Operator (,)

The comma operation (,) is used on two or more independent outflows that are incorporated where stand out statement is normal. At the point when the set of declarations must be assessed for a worth, just the rightmost articulation is considered.

Bitwise Operators

Bitwise operations include bitwise and (&), bitwise or (|), ~, ^, >> and <<. These operators adjust variables considering the bit designs that speak to the qualities they store.

Explicit Type Casting Operator

This operator permits you to change over a datum of an offered type to an alternate one. There are a few approaches to do this in C++. The most straightforward one, which has been inherited from the C dialect, is to go before the declaration to be changed over by the new type encased between enclosures (()).

Example

```
int i;
float f;
i = int ( f );
```

The code mentioned above declares two variables i and f. While i is an integer, f is a float. Directly assigning f to i will invoke a warning. Therefore, you need to typecast it. The third statement converts the flat variable's value to an integer and assigns the same to the integer variable.

Operator Precedence

You may have to create complex expressions. However, this may bring forth several questions. We may have a few questions about which operand is assessed first and which later. For instance, in this representation:

```
x = 5 – 4 + 3;
```

Ideally, a left to right evaluation is performed. However, operators follow a precedence order. The following table gives the order in which operations are performed.

Operator

Level

::

1

()

[]

--

▭

->

typeid

static_cast

dynamic_cast

const_cast

reinterpret_cast

2

--

!

sizeof

new

delete

3

*&

+-

(TYPE)

4

.* ->*

5

*/%

6

+-

7

<< >>

8

< > <= >=

9

== !=

10

&

11

^

12

|

13

&&

14

||

15

?:

16

= *= /= %= += -= >>= <<= &= ^= |=

17

,

18

This table describes the priority with which operators are evaluated if two or more of the operators mentioned here are used.

4

Basic Input / Output In C++

Utilizing the standard include and package library, we will have the capacity to interface with the client by printing messages on the screen and getting the client's information from the console. C++ utilizes a helpful deliberation called streams to perform output and input operations in successive media, for example, the screen or the console.

A stream is an item where a system can either embed or concentrate characters to/from it. We don't generally need to think about numerous determinations about the physical media connected with the stream - we just need to know it will acknowledge or give characters successively.

The standard C++ library incorporates the header document iostream, where the standard output and input stream items are pronounced.

Standard Output (cout)

Naturally, the standard output of a project is the screen, and the C++ stream item characterized to get to it is cout. cout is utilized as a part of conjunction with the insertion operator, which is composed as <<.

Sample Implementation:

cout << "This is C++";

Standard Input (cin).

The standard data gadget is generally the console. Standard input can be used in C++ by applying the operator of extraction (>>) on the cin stream. The operator must be trailed by the variable that will store the information that is going to be concentrated from the stream.

Sample Implementation

int x;

cin >> x;

Cin and Strings

We can utilize cin to get strings with the extraction operator (>>) as we do with principal information sort variables:

cin >> stringIn;

Nonetheless, as it has been said, cin extraction quits perusing when if discovers any clear space character. So, for this situation, we will have the capacity to get only single word for every extraction.

5

Control Structures

A system is normally not constrained to a straight grouping of guidelines. Amid its process, it may bifurcate, rehash code or take choices. For that reason, C++ gives control structures that serve to point out what must be carried out by our system, when and under which circumstances.

A large portion of the control structures that we will see in this area, oblige a bland explanation as a major aspect of its language structure. An announcement might be either a basic articulation (a straightforward guideline finishing with a semicolon) or a compound explanation (a few directions gathered in a square). In the case that we need the announcement to be a straightforward articulation, we don't have to wall it in braces ({}). Be that as it may in the case that we need the announcement to be a compound proclamation, it must be encased between braces ({}), framing a piece.

The if-else Construct

The construct 'if' defines a condition and a set of instructions. The if-block is executed in the case that the condition is satisfied.

Syntax of the if construct is as follows:

```
if (<condition>)
{
//Code
}
```

Here, condition is the articulation that is constantly assessed. On the off chance that this condition is true, code is executed. In the event that it is false, code is overlooked (not executed) and the system proceeds with directly after this contingent structure.

An extended version of the if-construct is the if-else construct. The syntax of this construct is as follows:

```
if (<condition>)
{
//Code If True
}
else
{
//Code If False
}
```

On the off chance that this condition is true, code-if-true is executed. In the event that it is false, code-if-true is overlooked (not executed) and the system proceeds to execute code-if-false.

Example:

```
if (a == 0)
{
cout<<”Value of a: 0“;
}
else
{
cout<<”Value of a is not 0“;
}
```

Loops

Loops have as reason to rehash a piece of code a specific number of times or if the while a condition is satisfied.

Syntax of the while construct:

```
while (<condition>)
{
//Code
}
```

Its usefulness is just to rehash articulation while the condition set in declaration is true.

Syntax of the do-while loop:

```
do
{
//Code
} while (<condition>);
```

Its usefulness is precisely the same as the while loop, aside from the condition in the do-while loop, which is assessed after the execution of code execution rather than in the recent past, allowing no less than one execution of explanation regardless of the possibility that condition is never satisfied.

The do-while loop is generally utilized when the condition that need to focus the end of the circle is resolved inside the circle explanation itself, as in the past case, where the client enter inside the piece is what is utilized to figure out whether the circle need to end.

Syntax of the for loop:

```
for (<initialization>; <condition>; <build>)
{
//Code
}
```

Its primary capacity is to execute code while condition stays valid, in the same way as the while loop. Anyway likewise, the for-loop gives particular areas to contain an instatement explanation and an increment/decrement proclamation. So, this loop is uniquely intended to perform a dreary activity with a counter, which is instated and expanded on every cycle.

It lives up to expectations in the accompanying way:

1. Initialization is executed

For the most part, it is an introductory value setting for a counter variable. This is executed just once.

1. Condition is checked

In the event that the condition is true, the loop proceeds. However, if the condition is false, the loop executes after executing the build condition.

1. Statement is executed

Of course, it could be either a single-line code or a braces-encased lines of code like, { }.

1. Finally, whatever is determined in the build field is executed and the loop returns to step 2.

Jump Statements

C++ supports several forms of jump statements. These statements are discussed below.

The break Statement

Utilizing break, we can leave a loop regardless of the possibility that the condition for its end is not satisfied. It could be utilized to end an unending circle, or to constrain it to end before its regular end. Case in point, we are going to stop the tally down before its regular end.

The Continue Statement

The continue statement causes the code to avoid whatever is left of the loop in the current emphasis as though the end of the code piece had been arrived at, making it hop to the begin of the accompanying cycle.

The goto Statement

The goto permits to make an outright hop to an alternate point in the code. You ought to utilize this peculiarity with alert. Subsequent to its execution causes an unqualified bounce overlooking any kind of settling limitations. The goal point is distinguished by a name, which is then utilized as a contention for the goto line. A name is made of a legitimate identifier took after by a colon (:).

The exit() Function

The exit() is a function available in the cstdlib library. It can be used to end the current execution with a particular code. The syntax of using this function is as follows:

```
void exit (int exitcode);
```

The exitcode is utilized by some working frameworks and may be utilized by calling functions. By tradition, an exitcode of 0 implies that the system completed typically and some other worth implies that some lapse or startling results happened.

Sample Implementation:

```
exit (0);
```

The Switch Construct

The grammar of the switch construct is a bit particular. Its objective is to check a few conceivable values for an interpretation. Something like what we did at the start of this section with the linking of a few if and else if instructions. The syntax of this construct is:

```
switch (<integer to be monitored>)
{
case value1:
```

```
//code
break;
case value2:
//code
break;
.
.
default:
//code
break;
}
```

The switch construct is a bit particular inside the C++ dialect in light of the fact that it does not use blocks. Instead, it uses labels. This strengthens us to put break code after the concerned lines of code that we need to be executed for a particular condition.

Sample Implementation:

```
int a;
cin >> a;
switch (a)
{
case 0:
cout <<"Entered value is 0";
break;
case 1:
cout << "Entered value is 1";
break;
default:
cout << "Value other than 0 and 1 entered by the user";
break;
}
```

This code asks the user to enter an integer. If the value entered is 0, case 0 code is executed. However, if 1 entered by the user, case 1 is executed. If the user enters a random value, the switch-case skips all cases, and executes the default case. It is customary to end the default case with a break statement.

Moreover, please note that if you skip the break statements, the system executes all the cases following the true case. For instance, if you skip the break statements in the above-mentioned code and the user enters 0, the system will execute all the cases. Therefore, all the three statements will be printed.

6

Functions

You can structure your code using functions and allows you to get to all the potential that organized programming can offer to you in C++. A function is a gathering of statements that is executed when it is called from some purpose of the project. The accompanying is its organization:

```
<data type> <function identifier> (<parameter1>, <parameter2>, ...)
{
//code
}
```

Here,

- Data type is the data type of the information returned by the function.
- Function identifier is the identifier by which it will be conceivable to call the function.
- Parameters (the same number of as required): Each parameter comprises of a data type and identifier combination. Parameters are declared in the same manner as regular variables are

declared. They permit to pass values from the calling function to the function when it is called. These parameters are, typically separated, by commas.

- Code statements form the body of the function. It is a piece of proclamations encompassed by props

Scope of Variables

The extent of variables pronounced inside a function or some other inward square is just their function or their code-block and can't be utilized outside of them. Consider the following example for better understanding of the scope concept.

```
void func1()
{
int a;
//code
}
void func2()
{
int b;
//code
}
```

In the sample code given above, the variable 'a' is available only inside func1 () where variable 'b' is available only inside func2 (). Hence, the extent of nearby variables is restricted to the block level in which they are declared. All things considered, we likewise have the likelihood to declare variables, which can have a global scope. These are obvious from any purpose of the code, inside and outside all functions. With a specific end goal to declare global variables, you just need to announce the variable outside any block or function. However, this location must be in the assemblage of the project.

Functions with Void Return Value

If you go back to the syntax of declaration of a function, you will see that the data type declares the data type of the value returned by the function. However, some functions may not return anything in which case you will give the data type as void.

Envision that we need to make a capacity function to demonstrate a message on the screen. We needn't bother about giving a return value. For this situation, we ought to utilize the void data type for the function. This is an uncommon specifier that shows nonattendance of type.

Void can likewise be utilized within the function's parameter rundown to unequivocally point out that we need the function to take no real parameters when it is called.

Values Passed by Reference and By Value

When calling a function with parameters, what have gone to the function were duplicates of their values. However, never the variables themselves are sent. Any changes made to the value of the variable inside the function are not reflected on the original variable. On the other hand, if a reference of the variable is sent to the function, the changes made to the variable inside the function reflect on the original variable as they are.

Default Values in Parameters

At the point when declaring a function, we can define a default value for each of the parameters. This quality will be utilized if the relating contention is left clear when calling the function. To do that, we basically need to utilize the task operator and a value for the variable in the function revelation. In the event that a value for that parameter is not passed when the function is called, the default value is utilized. However, in the event that a value is defined this default quality is disregarded and the passed value is utilized.

Overloaded Functions

In C++ two separate functions can have the same name if their parameter types or number are distinctive. That implies that you can give the same name to more than one function on the off chance that they have either an alternate number of parameters or diverse parameter data types.

A sample implementation is given below:

```
#include <iostream>
using namespace std;
float processnum (float x, float y)
{
return (x/y);
}
int processnum (int x, int y)
{
return (x+y);
}
int main () {
int a=2, b=2;
float c=4.0,m=4.0;
cout << processnum (a, b)<<endl;
cout << processnum (c, d)<<endl;
return 0;
}
```

For this situation we have declared and defined two functions with the same name processnum. One of them acknowledges two parameters of sort int and the other one acknowledges them of sort float. The compiler knows which one to bring in each one case by analyzing the data passed as values when the function is called. On the off chance that it is called with two ints as its parameters, it calls to the function that has two int parameters in its declaration. On the other hand, in the event that it is called with two floats, it will call the particular case that has two float parameters in its model.

In the first call to processnum(), the two parameters passed are of sort int. Subsequently, the function with the second declaration is called, which adds the two values and returns the result. However, the second call passes two parameters of sort float. So, the function with the first model is called. This one has an alternate conduct, which divides one parameter from the other. So, the conduct of a call to function relies on upon the sort of the parameters passed on the grounds that the function has been overloaded.

It is important to note that that a function can be overloaded in other ways as well and no less than one of its parameters must have an alternate data type.

Inline Functions

The inline specifier demonstrates to the compiler that inline substitution is desired for the concerned function. This does not change the conduct of a function itself. However, it is utilized to recommend to the compiler that the code produced by the body of the function must be embedded at the point the function is called, as opposed to being embedded just once and perform a general call to it, which for the most part includes some extra overhead in running time.

Standard Syntax:

```
inline <data type> <identifier> ( <parameters with their data types> )
{
//Code
}
```

Please note that the call is much the same as the call to

any other standard function. Also, you don't need to incorporate the inline word while calling the function. It just needs to be specified at the declaration-definition of the function.

Recursivity

Recursivity is the property that allows calling of functions without any input or external intervention. It is valuable for implementation of some functionality such as sorting or computing the factorial of numbers.

7

Arrays

An array is an arrangement of components of the same data type, put in sequential memory areas that might be exclusively referenced by using the following format:

arrayRef[i]

Here, arrayRef is any array and i can be any integer value, not greater than the number of elements in the array. This implies that, for instance, we can store 5 values of int type in an array without needing to pronounce 5 separate variables. All these are referenced using one identifier. Like a normal variable, an array must be declared before it is utilized. A normal affirmation for an exhibit in C++ is:

<data type> <identifier> [<number of elements>];

Here data type is the data type of the elements that the array will hold, identifier is a unique name given to the array and number of elements indicate the number of elements present in the array.

Example:

If you want to store five numbers of integer type, you

need to declare this structure using the following declaration:

int num [5];

Initializing Arrays

At the point when proclaiming a customary exhibit of array (inside a function, for instance), in the event that we don't tag else, its components won't be instated to any value naturally. So, their substance will be undetermined until we store some value in them. The components of global and static nature, then again, are naturally instated with their default values. Therefore, all the elements of global or static arrays are initialized to 0.

Accessing Elements Of The Array

In any purpose of a system in which an array is obvious, we can get to the value of any of its element independently as though it was a typical variable, accordingly having the capacity to both read and adjust its value. The configuration is as straightforward as:

<identifier> [<index>]

For example, if you wish to access the first element of array num, declared in the previous section, you must use the statement:

a = num [0];

In C++, it is linguistically right to surpass the substantial scope of records for a array. This can create issues, since getting to out-of-reach components don't result in gathering blunders yet can result in runtime slips. The motivation behind why this is permitted will be seen further ahead when we start to utilize pointers.

Multidimensional Arrays

Multidimensional arrays might be depicted as "array of arrays". Case in point, a bi-dimensional array might be envisioned as a bi-dimensional table made of components, every one of them of a same uniform information sort.

Multidimensional clusters are not restricted to two indexes (i.e., two measurements). They can contain the same number of records as required. However be watchful! The measure of memory required for a cluster quickly increments with each one increment.

Arrays as Parameters

At some point, we may need to pass an array to a function as a parameter. In C++, it is impractical to pass a complete square of memory by value as a parameter to a function. However, we are permitted to pass its address. In practice, this has very nearly the same impact and it is a much speedier and a more productive operation.

Keeping in mind the end goal to acknowledge arrays as parameters, the main thing that we need to do when declaring the function is to point out in its parameters the component kind of the array, an identifier and a couple of void sections [].

Character Sequences

As you may know, the C++ Standard Library executes an effective string class, which is extremely helpful to handle and control series of characters. On the other hand, on the grounds that strings are indeed arrangements of characters, we can speak to them likewise as plain arrays of char components.

Initialization of Null-Terminated Character Sequences

Since clusters of characters are normal arrays, they take after all their same standards. For instance, in the event that we need to introduce an array of characters with some foreordained arrangement of characters, we can do it much the same as any other. A sample implementation of this functionality is:

```
char name[] = { 'J', 'o', 'h', 'n', '\0' };
```

In this case, you could have declared a char array with

5 elements. While you can initialize char arrays in the manner shown above, you can perform the same function in a better manner using string literals.

Using null-terminated sequences of characters

The standard way of defining strings in C++ programming language is as a sequence of characters that are terminated with a null character (\0). This is the format used for string literals as well.

8

Pointers

We have as of now perceived how variables are seen as memory cells that could be gotten to utilizing their identifiers. Thusly, we didn't need to think about the physical area of our information inside memory. We basically utilized its identifier at whatever point we needed to allude to our variable.

The memory of your machine could be envisioned as a progression of memory cells, every one of the negligible sizes, which machines deal with (one byte). The memory cells are sequential in nature. Therefore, every element in this block is the same number as the past one in addition to one.

Reference Operator (&)

When we declare a variable, the measure of memory required is allocated for it at a particular area in memory (its memory address). We, by and large, don't heartily choose the accurate area of the variable inside the board of cells that we have envisioned the memory to be.

Fortunately, that is an undertaking naturally performed by the working framework at runtime. Be that as it may, sometimes, we may be intrigued about knowing the location where our variable is constantly put away during runtime so as to work with relative positions to it.

The address that spots a variable inside memory is the thing that we call a reference to that variable. This reference to a variable might be gotten by placing before the identifier of a variable an ampersand sign (&), known as reference operator, and which could be actually interpreted as "location of".

Dereference Operator (*)

We have quite recently seen that a variable, which stores a reference to an alternate variable, is known as a pointer. Utilizing a pointer, we can specifically get to the value put away in the variable, which it indicates. To do this, we basically need to place before the pointer's identifier a reference bullet (*), which goes about as dereference operator and that could be actually mean "value pointed by".

Contrast Between Reference and Dereference Operators

- Ampersand (&) is the reference operator and might be perused as "location of"
- Asterisk (*) is the dereference operator and might be perused as "quality pointed by"

Pointers and Arrays

The idea of array is really bound to the one of pointer. Actually, the identifier of a cluster is equal to the location of its first component, as a pointer is identical to the location of the first component that it indicates. Truth be told, they are the same idea.

The accompanying task operation would be legitimate:

p = num;

If p is a pointer and num is an array, both of the same type, p and numbers would be comparable and would have the same properties, after this statement. The main contrast is that we could change the value of pointer p by another, while numbers will dependably indicate the first of the different elements of a fixed data type with which it was characterized.

Hence, dissimilar to p, which is a conventional pointer, numbers is a array. Therefore, an array could be viewed as a consistent pointer. In this manner, the accompanying designation would not be substantial:

num = p;

Since numbers is an array, it works as a steady pointer, and we can't relegate values to constants.

Pointers to Pointers

C++ permits the utilization of pointers that indicate pointers, which in its turn, point to information (or even to different pointers). With a specific end goal to do that, we just need to include a bullet (*) for each one level of reference in their revelations.

Null Pointer

A null pointer is a customary pointer of any pointer, which has an exceptional value that demonstrates that it is not indicating any legitimate reference or memory address. This quality is the consequence of sort throwing the number value zero to any pointer sort.

Don't mistake null pointers for void pointers. A null pointer is a pointer that does not point to anything. On the other hand, a void pointer points to a location that contains a value of void type. One alludes to the value put away in the pointer itself and the other to the sort of information it indicates.

Pointers to Functions

C++ permits operations with pointers to functions.

The common utilization of this is for passing a capacity as a parameter to an alternate function, since these can't be passed dereferenced. To declare a pointer to a capacity, we need to announce it like the declaration of the function aside from that the name of the function is encased between enclosures () and a mark (*) is embedded before the name.

9

Dynamic Memory Allocation

As of recently, in all our examples, we had knew about the amount of memory we needed and we declared our variables, even arrays, on the basis of this estimate. As a result, we had all the memory required by the program allocated well in advance, before the execution of the code began.

At the same time, suppose you are faced with a situation where you require a variable measure of memory and this measure must be resolved amid runtime. For instance, in the case you require some client data to determine the essential measure of memory space required.

The answer to such a requirement is dynamic memory, for which C++ allows the operators new and delete.

Operators new and new []

With a specific end goal to ask for element memory, we utilize the operator new. A data type specifier trails the operator 'new'. However, if a grouping of more than one component is needed, the quantity of these can be mentioned inside sections []. It gives back a pointer to the start of the new square of memory distributed.

Syntax:

<pointer identifier> = new <data type>

<pointer identifier = new <type> [<number_of_elements>]

The main statement is utilized to dispense memory to contain one single component of the specified data type. The second one is utilized to allot an array of components of the specified data type, where number_of_elements is a whole number value speaking to the measure of these.

Operators delete and delete[]

Since the need of element memory is generally constrained to particular minutes inside a code, once it is no more required, it ought to be liberated so that the memory gets to be accessible again for different solicitations of element memory. This is the reason why the operator delete is provided.

Syntax:

delete <pointer identifier>;

delete [] <pointer identifier>;

The main representation ought to be utilized to erase memory apportioned for a solitary component, and the second one for memory allotted for array of components. The value passed as parameter to erase must be either a pointer to a memory apportioned with new, or a null pointer (on account of an null pointer, delete creates no impact).

10

Introduction to Object Oriented Programming: Classes

A class is an extended idea of an information structure, as opposed to holding just information. It can hold both functions and data. An object, on the other hand, is an instantiation of a class. Regarding variables, a class would be the type, and an object would be the variable.

Classes are by and large declared utilizing the keyword class, with the accompanying syntax:

```
class <className> {
accessSpecifier_1:
memberData;
memberFunction;
access_specifier_2:
memberData;
memberFunction;
} <objectName>;
```

Where className is an identifier for the class, objectName is a nonobligatory identifier of names for objects of this class. The assortment of the presentation can contain parts, which could be either data members or function statements, and alternatively get to specifiers.

Example:
int a;
Here, 'a' is an object of the int class.

Access Specifiers

All is fundamentally the same to the statement on information structures, aside from that we can now incorporate additionally functions and data parts, and this new thing called access specifier. A right to gain access or access specifier includes one of the accompanying three keywords: private, public or protected. These specifiers alter the right to gain entrance access to the members that fall under its scope.

- Private:

Such members of a class are available just from inside different members of the same class or from their companions.

- Protected

Such members are available from members of their same class and from their companions, additionally from parts of their inferred classes.

- Public

Such members are available from anyplace where the item is noticeable.

By default, all members of a class are private to access for all its members.

Example:
class myRectangle {

```
double a, b;
public:
void setValues (double, double);
double func (void);
} myRect;
```

In this example, a and b are private while functions setValues() and func() are public.

Constructors and Destructors

You, for the most part, need to introduce variables or allocate dynamic memory during the methodology of creation to clear up memory and to abstain from returning startling values during the execution of the program.

If you consider the previous example, had you sent 'a' and 'b' as parameters to a function without initializing them, the values taken by the function will be garbage. Your code will most likely give wrong results or crash abruptly.

Keeping in mind the end goal to keep away from that, a class can incorporate a unique function called constructor, which is naturally called at whatever point another object of this class is made. This constructor function must have the same name as the class, and can't have any return data type.

Example:

```
#include <iostream>
using namespace std;
class myRectangle {
double x, y;
public:
myRectangle (double, double);
double areaRect () {return (x*y);}
};
myRectangle :: myRectangle (double a, double b) {
```

```
x = a;
y = b;
}
int main ()
{
myRectangle rectx (1,2);
cout << "rect area: " << rectx.areaRect() << endl;
return 0;
}
```

The first statement in the main() instantiates the class myRectangle. The parameters passed with the creation of the object called the constructor function and initialize the dimensions of the rectangle to 1 and 2. Therefore, when the areaRect() is called, the function returns the correct value of area, 2.

Constructors can't be called unequivocally as though they were normal functions. They are just executed when another object of that class is made. You can likewise perceive how not one or the other, the constructor function (inside the class) nor the last constructor definition incorporate a return value, not even void.

The destructor satisfies the inverse usefulness. It is consequently called when an item needs to be demolished, either on the grounds that its extent of presence has completed (for instance, on the off chance that it was characterized as a nearby protest inside a function and the function closes) or in light of the fact that it is an article alertly appointed and it is discharged utilizing the operator delete.

The destructor must have the same name as the class. However, a tilde sign (~) is placed before the name and it should likewise give back no return value. The utilization of destructors is particularly suitable when an object uses dynamic memory amid its lifetime and right now of being annihilated, we need to discharge the memory that the item was designated.

Overloading Constructors

Like other functions, a constructor can likewise be overloaded with more than one function definitions that have the same name yet distinctive sorts or number of parameters. Keep in mind that for overloading to work, the compiler will call the one whose parameters match the values utilized as a part of the function call. On account of constructors, which are consequently called when an object is made, the one executed is the particular case that matches the values passed on the item assertion.

Default Constructor

In the event that you don't declare any constructors in a class definition, the compiler accepts the class to have a default constructor with no parameters. The compiler not just makes a default constructor for you on the off chance that you don't create your own.

It gives three extraordinary functions altogether that are certainly declared in the event that you don't declare your own. These are the copy constructor, the default destructor and the copy assignment operator.

The copy constructor and the copy assignment operator duplicate all the information contained in an alternate object to the members of the current object.

Pointers to Classes

It is flawlessly legitimate to make pointers that indicate classes. We essentially need to consider that once declared, a class turns into a substantial data type, so we can utilize the class name as the data type for the pointer.

Example:

myRectangle * pointerRect;

The pointerRect is a pointer to an object of class myRectangle.

As it happened with information structures, so as to allude specifically to a specific member of an object pointed by a pointer, we can utilize the arrow operator (->) of indirection.

11

Overloading Operators

C++ consolidates the alternative to utilize standard operators to perform operations with classes notwithstanding with major data types. C++ has a functionality that allows you to overload operators by planning classes ready to perform operations utilizing standard administrators.

To over-burden an operator with a specific end goal to utilize it with classes we proclaim operator functions, which are consistent functions whose names are the function keywords emulated by the operator sign that we need to overload. The arrangement is:

```
<data type> <operator> <operator sign>
(<parameters>)
{
//Code
}
```

Here you have an illustration that overloads the addition operator (+). We are going to make a class to store 2-D vectors and afterward, we are going to include two of them: a (2,4) and b (3,4). The addition of two 2-D vectors is an operation as basic as adding the two x directions to get the ensuing x direction. The result of this operation on the points 'a' and 'a' should be (2+3, 4+4), which is equal to (5, 8).

```
#include <iostream>
using namespace std;
class myVector {
public:
int a, b;
myVector () {};
myVector (int, int);
myVector operator + (myVector);
};
myVector :: myVector (int x, int y) {
a = x;
b = y;
}
myVector myVector :: operator+ (myVector myParam)
{ myVector tempo;
tempo.a = a + myParam.a;
tempo.b = b + param.b;
return (tempo);
}
int main () {
myVector x (2, 4);
myVector y (3, 4);
myVector z;
z = x + y;
cout << z.a << "," << z.b;
return 0;
}
```

Keyword this

The word this speaks of a pointer to the object whose member function is continuously executed. It is a pointer to the object itself.

It is additionally regularly utilized as a part of operator= function that returns objects by reference (keeping away from the utilization of impermanent objects). Taking after with the vector's illustrations seen before we could have composed an operator= capacity like this one.

Actually this capacity is very much alike to the code that the compiler creates verifiably for this class on the off chance that we do exclude an operator= part function to duplicate objects of this class.

Static Members

A class can contain static parts, either data or functions. Static data of a class are otherwise called "class variables", on the grounds that there is stand out novel values for all the objects of that same class. Their substance is not the same as one object of this class to an alternate.

Friend Functions

On a fundamental level, private members of a class can't be gotten to from outside the same class in which they are pronounced. Then again, this standard does not influence friend functions.

On the off chance that we need to proclaim an outside function as friend of a class, in this manner permitting this capacity to have admittance to the private and secured members of this class, we do it by proclaiming a model of this outer capacity inside the class, and placing the keyword friend before it.

Example:

```
#include <iostream>
using namespace std;
class myRectangle {
int x, y;
public:
void setValues (int, int);
```

```
int func () {return (x * y);} friend myRectangle copy (myRectangle);
};
void myRectangle :: setValues (int a, int b) {
x = a;
y = b;
}
myRectangle copy (myRectangle rectParam) {
myRectangle rects;
rects.x = rectParam.x*2;
rects.y = rectParam.y*2;
return (rects);
}
int main () {
myRectangle rectx, recty;
rectx.setValues (2,3);
recty = copy (rectx);
cout << recty.func();
return 0;
}
```

The copy function is a friend function of myRectangle. From inside that function, we have possessed the capacity to get to the private members of the class, 'x' and 'y'. Recognize that not one or the other in the statement of copy() nor in its later use in principle() have we considered copy a part of class myRectangle. It isn't! It essentially has entry to its private and secured members without being a part of the class.

The friend function can serve, for instance, to direct operations between two separate classes. For the most part, the utilization of friend function is out of an item arranged programming technique, so at whatever point conceivable it is better to utilize parts of the same class to perform operations with them.

Friend Classes

Generally as we have the likelihood to declare a friend function capacity, we can likewise declare a class as friend of another, allowing that top of the line access to the ensured and private members of the second one.

Example

```
#include <iostream>
using namespace std;
class mySquare;
class myRectangle {
int x, y;
public:
int myArea () {return (x * y);}
void convert (mySquare a);
};
class mySquare {
private:
int x;
public:
void setSide (int a)
{side=a;}
friend class myRectangle;
};
void myRectangle::convert (mySquare a) {
x = a.x;
y = a.x;
}
int main () {
mySquare sqr;
myRectangle rect;
sqr.setSide(4);
rect.convert(sqr);
cout << rect.myArea();
return 0;
```

```
}
```

In this illustration, we have declared myRectangle as a companion of mySquare so that myRectangle functions could have entry to the ensured and private members of mySquare, all the more solidly to Csquare::x, which portrays the side of the square.

12

Inheritance between Classes

A key feature of C++ classes is inheritance, which permits you to make classes that are inferred from different classes. So, they naturally incorporate some of its "parent's" members, in addition to its own.

Classes that are inferred from others inherit all the available parts of the base class. That implies that if a base class incorporates a part A and we determine it to an alternate class with an alternate part called B, the determined class will contain both parts A and B.

To determine a class from an alternate, we utilize a colon (:) as a part of the revelation of the inferred class utilizing the accompanying arrangement:

class <derived class name>: public <base_class_name>

{

//Code

};

Where derived_class_name is the name of the inferred class and base_class_name is the name of the class on which it is based. The public specifier may be supplanted by any of alternate access specifiers protected and private. This access specifier portrays the base access level for the parts that are inherited from the base class.

```
#include <iostream>
using namespace std;
class myPol {
protected:
double x, y;
public:
void setValues (double a, double b)
{ x = a; y = b;}
};
class myRect: public myPol {
public:
double myArea ()
{
return (x * y);
}
};
class myTri: public myPol {
public:
int myArea ()
{
return (x * y/ 2);
}
};
int main () {
myRect rect;
myTri trgl;
rect.setValues (4,5);
trgl.setValues (4,5);
cout << rect.myArea() << endl;
cout << trgl.myArea() << endl;
return 0;
```

}

The objects of the classes, myRectangle and myTriangle, each one contain members inherited from myPolygon. These are: x, y and setValues().

The protected access specifier is like private. Its contrast happens actually with inheritance. At the point when a class inherits from another, the parts of the inherited class can get access to the protected members inherited from the base class, however not its private members.

Since we needed x and y to be public from parts of the inferred classes myRectangle and myTriangle and not just by parts of myPolygon, we have utilized protected rather than private.

What Is Inherited From The Base Class

On a basic level, an inherited class inherits each member of a base class with the exception of:

- Constructor
- Destructor
- Operator=() members
- Friends

Although, the destructors and constructors of the base class are not inherited themselves, the destructor and default constructor are constantly called when another object of an inherited class is made or destroyed. In the event that the base class has no default constructor or you need that an overload constructor is called when another inherited object is made, you can detail it in every constructor meaning of the determined class:

<derived constructor name> (<parameters>) : <base constructor name> (<parameters>) {

//Code

}

Multiple Inheritance

There is a provision for a class to inherit from multiple classes in C++. This can be carried out, by separating the base classes, with commas in the class declaration. Case in point, in the event that we had a particular class to print on screen (myOutput) and we needed our classes myRectangle and myTriangle to likewise inherit its members notwithstanding those of myPolygon we could compose them accordingly.

13

Implementing Polymorphism

Before getting into this segment, it is prescribed that you have a legitimate understanding of pointers and class inheritance. In the event that any of the accompanying explanations appear unusual to you, you ought to audit the showed segments:

Pointers to base class

One of the key peculiarities of inherited classes is that a pointer to an inferred class is sort good with a pointer to its base class. Polymorphism is the craft of exploiting this straightforward however compelling and flexible peculiarity that brings Object Oriented Methodologies to its maximum capacity.

Virtual Members

A part of a class that could be reclassified in its inferred classes is known as a virtual member. With a specific end goal to declare a part of a class as virtual, we must place before its statement the keyword virtual.

What the virtual key word does is that it permits a part of a determined class with the same name as one in the base class to be properly called from a pointer, and all the more accurately when the kind of the pointer is a pointer to the base class yet is indicating an object of the inferred class.

Abstract Base Class

The fundamental distinction between a theoretical base class and a customary polymorphic class is that in light of the fact that in conceptual base classes no less than one of its parts needs usage, we can't make cases (items) of it. Be that as it may a class that can't instantiate objects is not completely futile. We can make pointers to it and exploit all its polymorphic capabilities.

Virtual members and dynamic classes stipend C++ the polymorphic qualities that make item situated programming such a helpful instrument in huge activities. Obviously, we have seen exceptionally basic employments of these features, however these peculiarities could be connected to exhibits of items or progressively apportioned objects.

14

Function Templates and Class Templates

Function templates are unique functions that can work with non-specific data types. This permits us to make a function layout whose usefulness could be adjusted to more than one sort or class without rehashing the whole code for each one sort.

In C++, this could be attained utilizing template parameters. A template parameter is an uncommon sort of parameter that might be utilized to pass a type as parameter: much the same as normal parameters could be utilized to pass values to a function, format parameters permit to pass likewise sorts to a function. These templates can utilize these parameters as though they were some other customary data type.

The syntax used for this is as follows:

template <typename identifier> function_declaration;

template <class identifier> function_declaration;

Both the statements written above have the same meaning and effect. The only difference lies in the use of keywords, typename or class.

Example:

To illustrate the concept of function templates, let us create a template that returns the higher value of the two parameters provided to it.

```
template <class eType>
eType GetMaxVal (eType x, eType y) {
return (x>y?x:y);
}
int a,b;
GetMaxVal <int> (a,b);
```

In this example, a template parameter, eType has been used, which is symbolic of the data type that has not be specified as yet. This parameter can be used as a data type for the function just like any other data type. The GetMaxVal function template returns the greater value of the two parameters provided to it. In order to call this function template, you need to make the following function call.

```
<function name> <data type> (<parameters>);
```

For example, if you wish to call GetMaxVal for int, then you can make the following call:

```
GetMaxVal <int>(a, b)
```

Here, ‘a’ and ‘b’ are any two integers.

Sample Code:

```
#include <iostream>
using namespace std;
template <class X>
X GetMaxVal (X a, X b)
{
X val;
result = (a>b)? a : b;
return (result);
}
```

```
int main () {
int x = 1, y = 2, z;
long i=21, j=10, k;
z=GetMaxVal<int>(x,y);
k=GetMaxVal<long>(i,j);
cout << z << endl;
cout << k << endl;
return 0;
}
```

In this example, X is used as a data type. However, you can use a name you like. The two function calls to GetMaxVal are for different data types, int and long. It has, in fact, being used as a data type for creating new objects as well. The output of the function is the of the data type for which the function is being called.

In the above example, the compiler will implicitly call the template function with int if you call the function with parameters 'x' and 'y'. However, if you call the function with long parameters, the compiler will call the template function for long. There is no need to specify <int> or <long> in these cases as the parameters used for calling the template function have been declared already. Therefore, the following function call shall suffice:

```
GetMaxVal (x, y);
```

However, please note that you cannot use parameters of different types in the function call. If you need to do something of this sort, then you must define two data types like X in the template function.

Class templates

Just like function templates, you can also choose to write class templates. The members of this class can use the user-defined type as parameters.

```
template <class myType>
```

```
class myNums {
myType vals [2];
public:
myNums (myType one, myType two)
{
vals[0]=first; vals[1]=second; }
};
```

Class templates use members with data types, which are defined by the user. The template class illustrated above creates an object, which can store two numbers. These two numbers can be of any data type. The user-defined data type myType is used to indicate this type. The class template can be used for creating object pairs of different types in the following manner:

```
myNums<int> myintnum (334, 45);
myNums<double> myintfloat (1.0, 4.25);
```

Sample Code:

```
#include <iostream>
using namespace std;
template <class myType>
class myNum {
myType x, y;
public:
myNums (myType one, myType two)
{x=one; y=two;}
myType getMaxVal ();
};
template <class myType>
myType myNums<myType>::getMaxVal ()
{
T retValue;
retValue = x>y? x : y;
return retValue;
}
```

```
int main () {
myNums <int> myOb (125, 27);
cout << myOb.getMaxVal();
return 0;
}
```

15

Namespaces

Namespaces permit you to club elements like classes, functions and objects under a name. Thusly the worldwide extension could be separated in "sub-scopes", every unified with its name.

Syntax for namespace:

```
namespace <identifier name>
{
//elements
}
```

Where identifier is any substantial identifier and elements is the situated of classes, functions and objects that are incorporated inside the namespace. The usefulness of namespaces is particularly helpful in the case that there is plausibility that a global function or object utilizes the same identifier as another, bringing about redefinition blunders.

Example:

```
namespace eNamespace
{
int x, y;
```

```
}
eNamespace::x
eNamespace::y
#include <iostream>
using namespace std;
namespace sample1
{
double myvar = 5;
}
namespace sample2
{
double myvar = 3.1416;
}
int main () {
cout << sample1::var;
cout<<"\n";
cout << sample2::var;
cout<<"\n";
return 0;
}
```

For this situation, there are two variables with the same name: myvar. One is defined inside the namespace sample1 and the other one in sample2. No redefinition blunders happen because of namespaces.

The using Keyword

The word using is utilized to present a name from a namespace to interfere with another of the same name in another namespace.

Example:

```
#include <iostream>
using namespace std;
namespace sample1
{
double x = 0.1;
```

```
double y = 1.5;
}
namespace sample2
{
double x = 1.1123;
double y = 5.645;
}
int main () {
using sample1::x;
using sample2::y;
cout << x;
cout<<"\n";
cout << y;
cout<<"\n";
cout << sample1::y;
cout<<"\n";
cout << sample2::x;
cout<<"\n";
return 0;
}
```

Recognize how in this code, x (without any name qualifier) alludes to sample1::x while y alludes to sample2::y, precisely as our utilizing assertions have defined. In any case we have admittance to sample1::y and sample2::x utilizing their completely qualified names. The keyword can likewise be utilized as an order to present a whole namespace:

Example:

```
#include <iostream>
using namespace std;
namespace sample1
{
int x = 56;
int y = 70;
```

```
}
namespace sample2
{
double x = 1.1125;
double y = 5.5567;
}
int main () {
using namespace sample1;
cout << x;
cout<<"\n";
cout << y;
cout<<"\n";
cout << sample2::x;
cout<<"\n";
cout << sample2::y;
cout<<"\n";
return 0;
}
```

This will print the sample1 values followed by the sample2 values.

Namespaces are valid only within the blocks that they are declared. Case in point, in the event that we had the proposition to first utilize the objects of one namespace and afterward those of another, we could do something like:

Example:

```
#include <iostream>
using namespace std;
namespace sample1
{
double x = 0;
}
namespace sample2
{
```

```
double x = 1.1216;
}
int main () {
{
using namespace sample1;
cout << x
cout<<"\n";
}
{
using namespace sample2;
cout << x
cout<<"\n";
}
return 0;
}
```

This code will print the x value for sample1 and then print the x value for sample2.

Namespace Aliasing

We can declare alias names for existing namespaces as per the accompanying configuration:

```
namespace newName = presentName;
```

Namespace std

All the documents in the C++ standard library proclaim every last bit of its elements inside the std namespace. That is the reason why all programs have the statement that specifies that the code is using namespace 'std 'at the beginning of the program.

16

Exceptions Handling

Exception handling gives an approach to respond to extraordinary circumstances (like runtime blunders) in our system by exchanging control to unique capacities called handlers. However, in order to handle exceptions, you are required to put your code in the exception inspection.

At the point when an uncommon situation emerges inside that block, an exemption is tossed that exchanges the control to the special case handler. In the event that no special case is tossed, the code proceeds with regularly and all handlers are overlooked.

An exception is thrown by utilizing the throw keyword from inside the attempt piece. Handlers are declared with the keyword catch, which must be put promptly after the try block:

```
#include <iostream>
using namespace std;
int main () {
try
{
throw 0;
```

```
}
catch (int e)
{
cout << "Catch Block Entered!"
cout << "Exception ID:" << e;
cout<<"\n";
}
return 0;
}
```

This code output the statement in the cout along with the exception ID.

The exception handler is announced with the catch keyword. As should be obvious, it starts after the end of the try square. The catch arrangement is like a consistent function that dependably has no less than one parameter. The sort of this parameter is extremely imperative, since the kind of the contention passed by the throw outflow is checked against it, and just in the case they match, the exemption is gotten.

We can chain different handlers (try outflows), every unified with an alternate parameter sort. Just the handler that matches its write with the contention tagged in the toss proclamation is executed.

After a special case has been taken care of the project execution continues after the try-catch, not after the throw!

Specifications of Exceptions

At the point when declaring a function, we can restrict the exception type. It may specifically or by implication throw by affixing a throw addition to the function declaration.

```
float myFunction (char myParam) throw (int);
```

This declares a function myFunction, which takes one argument and returns a float. The main exception that this capacity may throw is a special case of int. In the event that it throws a special case with an alternate sort, either specifically or in a roundabout way, then an int-type handler cannot catch the same.

In the event that this throw specifier is left vacant with no type, this implies the function is not permitted to throw exceptions. Functions with no specifier are permitted to throw special cases of any type.

Standard Exceptions

The C++ Standard library gives a base class particularly intended to declare objects that are thrown as exceptions. These are present in the header file, <exception>.

It is prescribed to incorporate all dynamic memory designations inside a try obstruct that gets this kind of exception to perform a cleaning activity rather than an irregular end, which is the thing that happens when this type of special case is thrown and not caught.

17

Typecasting

Changing over an interpretation of a given data type into an alternate data type is known as type casting. We have as of now seen a few approaches to type cast.

Implicit Conversion

Certain changes don't require any operator. They are naturally performed when a value is replicated to another sort. The value of 'a' has been elevated from short to int and we have not needed to determine any data type casting operator. This is known as a implicit change.

Implicit changes influence fundamental data types, and permit transformations, for example, the transformations between numerical types (short to int, int to float) and some pointer changes. Some of these changes may intimate a loss of exactness, which the compiler can motion with a cautioning. This could be kept away from with an express transformation.

Implied transformations likewise incorporate constructor or operator changes, which influence classes that incorporate particular constructors or administrator capacities to perform transformations.

Explicit Conversion

C++ is a solid programming language. Numerous transformations, exceptionally those that suggest an alternate elucidation of the value, require an explicit transformation. We have as of now seen two documentations for this type of typecasting namely, c-like and functional.

The usefulness of these conversions is sufficient for most needs with essential data types. Notwithstanding, these operators might be connected randomly on classes and pointers to classes, which can prompt code that while being linguistically right can result in runtime blunders.

Conventional typecasting permits to change over any pointer into whatever other pointer sort, freely of the sorts they indicate. The ensuing call to a member come about will create either a run-time lapse or a surprising result.

Keeping in mind the end goal to control these sorts of transformations between classes, we have four particular operators: reinterpret_cast, dynamic_cast, const_cast and static_cast. Their functionality is explained below.

dynamic_cast

dynamic_cast might be utilized just with pointers and references to protests. Its design is to guarantee that the aftereffect of the change is a legitimate complete object of the asked for the class. Therefore, dynamic_cast is effective when we cast a class to one of its base classes.

static_cast

static_cast can perform transformations between pointers and related classes, not just from the inferred class to its base, additionally from a base class to its determined. This guarantees that at any rate the classes are perfect if the correct object is changed over. However, no wellbeing check is performed amid runtime to check if the item being changed over is right.

Along these lines, it is dependent upon the developer to

guarantee that the change is sheltered. On the other side, the overhead of the sort security checks of dynamic_cast is dodged. static_cast can likewise be utilized to perform whatever other non-pointer change that could be performed verifiably, as for instance standard transformation between fundamental data types.

reinterpret_cast

reinterpret_cast changes over any pointer type to whatever other pointer type, even of random classes. The operation result is a basic double duplicate of the value from one pointer to the next. All pointer transformations are permitted: not the element pointed or the pointer sort itself is checked.

It can likewise cast pointers to or from whole number sorts. The configuration in which this whole number value speaks to a pointer is stage particular. The main surety is that a pointer cast to a number sort expansive enough to completely contain it, is conceded to have the capacity to be thrown over to a substantial pointer.

The changes that might be performed by reinterpret_-cast, however not by static_cast have no particular uses in C++ are low-level operations, whose understanding brings about code which is by and large framework particular, and subsequently non-versatile.

This is substantial C++ code, despite the fact that it doesn't bode well, since now we have a pointer that indicates an object of a contradictory class, and accordingly dereferencing it is risky.

const_cast

This kind of throwing controls the constant-ness of an object, either to be set or to be uprooted.

typeid

typeid permits to check the kind of an outflow: typeid (interpretation)

This operator gives back a reference to a object of sort type_info that is characterized in the standard header record <typeinfo>. This returned quality might be contrasted and another utilizing administrators == and != or can serve to acquire an invalid ended character succession speaking to the information sort or class name by utilizing its name() part.

At the point when typeid is connected to classes, typeid utilizes the RTTI to stay informed regarding the type of element items. At the point when typeid is connected to a code whose type is a polymorphic class, the result is the kind of the most determined complete object.

18

Preprocessor directives

The lines included in the code of our example that are not program code yet mandates for the preprocessor are called processor directives. These lines are constantly used and can be identified with a hash sign (#). The preprocessor is executed before the genuine assemblage of code starts. In this way, the preprocessor processes all these mandates before any code is created by the announcements.

These preprocessor mandates expand just over a solitary line of code. When a newline character is found, the preprocessor mandate is considered to end. No semicolon (;) is normally used at the end of a preprocessor mandate. The main way a preprocessor order can stretch out through more than one line is by going before the newline character at the end of the line by an oblique punctuation line (\).

Macro definitions

To characterize preprocessor macros we can utilize #define. Its syntax is:

#define <identifier name> <substitution code>

At the point when the preprocessor finds this directive,

it replaces any event of identifier in whatever remains of the code by substitution. This substitution might be a code, an announcement, a piece or just anything. The preprocessor does not comprehend C++. It basically replaces any event of identifier by substitution.

Example:

#define getMaxVal(x,y) x>y?x:y

This would supplant any event of getMaxVal and its two parameters, by the substitution interpretation, additionally supplanting every contention by its identifier, precisely as you would expect on the off chance that it was a function.

Macros are not influenced by structure. A macro endures until it is unclear with the #undef preprocessor order. Function macro definitions acknowledge two unique operators (# and ##) in the substitution sequence. If the administrator # is utilized before a parameter is utilized as a part of the substitution arrangement, that parameter is supplanted by a string strict (as though it were encased between quotes)

Conditional Directives

These mandates permit to incorporate or toss some piece of the code of a project if a certain condition is met.

#ifdef permits a segment of a project to be aggregated just if the macro that is

#ifndef serves for the precise inverse: the code in the middle of #ifndef and #endif mandates is just arranged if the indicated identifier has not been long ago characterized.

The #if, #else and #elif (i.e., "else if") orders serve to indicate some condition to be met in place for the bit of code they encompass to be gathered. The condition that takes after #if or #elif can just assess steady statements, including macro representations.

The entire structure of #if, #elif and #else binded mandates closes with #endif.

Line Control (#line)

When we direct a system and some blunder happen amid the accumulating process, the compiler demonstrates a lapse message with references to the name of the record where the mistake happened and a line number, so it is simpler to discover the code producing the slip.

The #line order permits us to control both things, the line numbers inside the code documents and the record name that we need that shows up when a lapse happens. Its syntax is:

#line number "filename"

Here, number is the new line number that will be doled out to the following code line. The line number of progressive lines will be expanded one by one starting here on.

"filename" is a nonobligatory parameter that permits to reclassify the document name that will be demonstrated. For instance:

File Inclusions

This mandate has likewise been utilized diligently as a part of different areas of this exercise. At the point when the preprocessor finds a #include order, it replaces it by the whole content of the defined record. There are two approaches to determine a record to be incorporated.

The main contrast between both representations is the spots (indexes) where the compiler is going to search for the record. In the first situation, where the document name is tagged between quotes, the record is looked first in the same catalog that incorporates the record containing the mandate. On the off chance that that it is not there, the compiler seeks the document in the default indexes where it is arranged to search for the standard header records.

On the off chance that the document name is encased

between point sections <>, the record is sought straightforwardly where the compiler is arranged to search for the standard header documents. Consequently, standard header records are normally included in edge sections, while other particular header documents are incorporated utilizing quotes.

Pragma Directives

This order is utilized to define assorted alternatives to the compiler. These alternatives are particular for the stage and the compiler you utilization. Look through the manual or the reference of your compiler for more data on the conceivable parameters that you can characterize with #pragma. On the off chance that the compiler does not help a particular contention for #pragma, it is disregarded - no slip is created.

19

C++ Standard Library - Input / Output with files

C++ gives the accompanying classes to perform output and input of characters to/from records:

- ofstream: Stream class to edit on documents
- ifstream: Stream class to read from documents
- fstream: Stream class to both read and edit from/to documents.

These classes are inferred straightforwardly or in a roundabout way from the classes, ostream and istream. We have effectively utilized objects whose types were these classes: cin is an object of class istream and cout is an object of class ostream.

Therefore, we have as of now been utilizing classes that are identified with our record streams. Furthermore indeed, we can utilize our document streams the same way we are now used to utilize cin and cout, with the main distinction that we need to partner these streams with physical records.

Example:

```
#include <iostream>
#include <fstream>
using namespace std;
int main () {
ofstream newFile;
newFile.open ("sample.txt");
newFile << "Editing this file.\n";
newFile.close();
return 0;
}
```

Writing To Document

This code makes a document called sample.txt and supplements a sentence into it in the same way we are utilized to do with cout, yet utilizing the record stream newFile.

Opening Files

The main operation for the most part performed on an object of one of these classes is to partner it to a genuine record. This system is known as to open a document. An open document is spoken to inside a system by a stream (an instantiation of one of these classes, in the past illustration this was myFile) and any operation performed on this stream object will be connected to the physical record related to it.

With a specific end goal to open a record with a stream object, we utilize its function open():

open (filename, mode);

Here, filename is the name of the file. Modes are given below for reference:

- ios::out - open for yield operations.
- ios::in - open for data operations.
- ios::ate - set the starting position at the end of the file.

- ios::binary - open in double mode.
- ios::trunc - In the event that the document opened for yield operations officially existed in the recent past, its past substance is erased and supplanted by the new one.
- ios::app - all yield operations are performed at the end of the document.

All these banners might be consolidated utilizing the bitwise administrator OR (|). Case in point, in the event that we need to open the record example.bin in binary mode to include information we could do it by the accompanying call to open():

Every one of the open() function of the classes ifstream, ofstream and fstream has a default mode that is utilized if the document is opened without a second operator. For ofstream and ifstream classes, ios::out and ios::in are naturally and individually accepted, regardless of the fact that a mode that does exclude them is passed as second parameter to the open() function.

The default value is just connected if the function is called without pointing out any quality for the mode parameter. On the off chance that the function is called with any value in that parameter the default mode is overridden, not joined.

Document streams opened in twofold mode perform output and input operations freely of any configuration parameters. Non-binary records are known as content documents, and a few interpretations may happen because of arranging of some exceptional characters (like newline and carriage return characters).

Since the first errand that is performed on a document stream article is for the most part to open a record, these three classes incorporate a constructor that consequently calls the open() function and has literally the same parameters as this part. Consequently, we could likewise have announced the past myfile protest and directed the same opening operation in our past case by composing:

```
ofstream myfile ("example.bin", ios::out | ios::app | ios::binary);
```

Joining item development and stream opening in a solitary explanation. Both structures to open a document are legitimate and proportionate. To check if a record stream was fruitful opening a document, you can do it by calling to part is_open() with no contentions. This function gives back a bool estimation of valid in the case that without a doubt the stream item is connected with an open record, or false overall:

Closing Files

When we are done with our operations on a record, we should close it so that its assets ended up accessible once more. So as to do that we need to call the stream's close() function. This function takes no parameters, and what it does is to flush the related handles and close the document:

```
newFile.close();
```

When this function is called, the stream object might be utilized to open an alternate record, and the document is accessible again to be opened by different methods. In the event that that an item is destructed while still connected with an open document, the destructor naturally calls close().

Text Files

Content document streams are those where we do exclude the ios::binary hail in their opening mode. These records are intended to store content and consequently all values that we enter or yield from/to them can endure some designing changes, which don't fundamentally compare to their strict binary value.

Notwithstanding eof(), which checks if the end of document has been arrived at, other functions exist to check the state of a stream (every one of them give back a bool value). In addition, there are several other functions like bad(), good() and eof() are available.

With a specific end goal to reset the state flags checked by any of these functions, we have recently seen we can utilize clear(), which takes no parameters.

The get and put Stream Pointers

All i/o streams have, no less than, one inward stream pointer. ifstream, in the same way as istream, has a pointer known as the get pointer that indicates the component to be perused in the following information operation.

- Returns true if a perusing or composing operation fizzles. For instance, in the case that we attempt to keep in touch with a document that is not open for composing or if the gadget where we attempt to compose has no space cleared out.
- Returns valid in the same cases as bad (), additionally in the case that an organization mistake happens, in the same way as when an in sequential order character is concentrated when we are attempting to peruse a number.
- Returns true if a record open for perusing has arrived at the end.

It is the most nonexclusive state flag: it returns false in the same cases in which calling any of the past capacities would return genuine.

ofstream, in the same way as ostream, has a pointer known as the put pointer that indicates the area where the following component must be composed. At last, fstream, inherits both, the get and the put pointers, from iostream (which is itself determined from both istream and ostream). These inner stream pointers that indicate the perusing or composing areas inside a stream could be controlled utilizing the accompanying functions:

tellg() and tellp()

These two functions have no parameters and return a value of the pos_type, which is a whole number data type indicative of the current position of the get stream pointer (on account of tellg) or the put stream pointer (on account of tellp).

seekg() and seekp()

These functions permit us to change the position of the get and put stream pointers. Both are overloaded with two separate models. The principal model is:

```
seekg ( position );
seekp ( position );
```

Utilizing this model, the stream pointer is changed to indisputably the position (checking from the earliest starting point of the record). The sort for this parameter is the same as the one returned by capacities tellg and tellp: the part sort pos_type, which is whole number value.

The other model for these capacities is:

```
seekg ( balance, heading );
seekp ( balance, heading );
```

Utilizing this model, the position of the get or put pointer is situated to a balanced value with respect to some particular point controlled by the parameter course. Balance is of the data type off_type, which is additionally a number. Furthermore, bearing is of sort seekdir, which is a listed sort (enum) that decides the point from where balanced is tallied from, and that can take any of the accompanying qualities:

The accompanying case utilizes the part capacities we have recently seen to acquire the measure of a document:

- ios::beg - offset checked from the earliest starting point of the stream
- ios::curoffset - checked from the current position of the stream pointer
- ios::end - offset checked from the end of the stream

Binary Files

In binary records, to enter and output information with the extraction and insertion operators (<< and >>) and functions like getline is not effective, since we don't have to organization any information, and information may not utilize the partition codes utilized by content documents to independent components. Record streams incorporate two functions particularly intended to output and input information successively: write and read.

Syntax:

```
write ( memoryBlock, size );
read ( memoryBlock, size );
```

The type of memoryBlock is "pointer to char" (char*), and indicates the location of a cluster of bytes where the read information components are put away or from where the information components to be composed are taken. The size parameter is a whole number esteem that points out the quantity of characters to be perused or composed from/to the memory square.

Example:

```
#include <fstream>
#include <iostream>
using namespace std;
char * memoryBlock;
```

```
ifstream::pos_type size;
int main () {
ifstream newFile ("sample.bin", ios::in|ios::binary|ios::ate);
if (myFile.is_open())
{
mySize = newFile.tellg();
memoryBlock = new char [size];
newFile.seekg (0, ios::beg);
newFile.read (memblock, size);
newFile.close();
cout << "the complete document substance is in memory"; delete[] memoryBlock;
}
else
cout << "Not able to open document";
return 0;
}
```

In this illustration the whole document is perused and put away in a memory square.

Buffers and Synchronization

When we work with document streams, these are related to an inward support of type streambuf. This buffer is a memory block that is a intermediary between the stream and the physical record. The flushing of buffer compels it to write all the data available on it to the physical memory if the stream is output and free the memory if the stream is input. This process is called synchronization. It can be explicitly performed by calling the function sync() or with the help of manipulators.

Appendix

List of reserved keywords is as follows:

- auto
- asm
- break
- bool
- catch
- case
- class
- char
- const_cast
- const
- default
- continue
- do
- delete
- dynamic_cast
- double
- enum
- else

- export
- explicit
- false
- extern
- for
- float
- goto
- friend
- inline
- if
- long
- int
- namespace
- mutable
- operator
- new
- protected
- private
- register
- public
- return, short
- reinterpret_cast
- sizeof
- signed
- static_cast
- static
- switch
- struct
- this
- template
- true
- throw
- typedef
- try

- typename
- typeid
- unsigned
- union
- virtual
- using
- volatile
- void
- while
- wchar_t

In addition to the above-mentioned, there are some other operators that are also reserved under special conditions. These include:

- and_eq
- and
- bitor
- bitand
- not
- compl
- or
- not_eq
- xor
- or_eq
- xor_eq

Some compilers may also have some additional reserved keywords. You may read the compiler documentation for more information.

www.ingramcontent.com/pod-product-compliance
Lightning Source LLC
La Vergne TN
LVHW052307060326
832902LV00021B/3752

9781952964602